"Is that 'L' as in Rome?"
"No, it's 'R' as in London."

GEMS OF JAPANIZED ENGLISH

A lighthearted
but unabashedly affectionate
portrait of the Japanese

Miranda Kenrick

"Is that 'L' as in Rome?"
"No, it's 'R' as in London."

GEMS OF JAPANIZED ENGLISH

illustrated by Motomi Naito

YENBOOKS are published and distributed by
the Charles E. Tuttle Company, Inc.
with editorial offices at
2–6 Suido 1-chome, Bunkyo-ku, Tokyo, Japan

Library of Congress Catalog Card No. 88–50779
International Standard Book No. 0–8048–1555–0

First printing, 1988
Fourth printing, 1989

Printed in Japan

Contents

Foreword

IT WAS AROUND NOON one Sunday that I was in line at the American Club's buffet brunch table. I did that particular brunch almost every Sunday during the years my wife, Sarah, and I lived in Japan, not so much because everything laid out there tasted good (it did), but more because it *looked* good—better than anything I was likely to see while working around the local countryside during the coming week.

You know what I mean, I'm sure. Nothing spread on that buffet table was moving, and all the vegetables were near the same familiar colors I remembered from back in Cleveland. And the American Club's soups were always either cloudy or clear, never half and half like native varieties.

Anyway, on the particular Sunday I'm talking about, I was lined up behind two just-off-the-plane newcomers who were comparing problems that they had dealt with—or thought they had dealt with—during the previous week in Tokyo. "There's no two ways about it," one of them decided. "The problem here is the language."

When I heard that observation, I was positive they had just arrived. If they had been in Japan more than seven days, they would have known that there *are* two ways about it, and that's why language is definitely the problem.

Actually, there are four ways about the problem. That's because there are two languages involved—Japanese and English. There are also, in turn, two Japanese languages. There's the one the Japanese speak, and then there's the one those of us foreigners who have taken Japanese lessons speak.

Same goes for English. There's the English we foreigners speak, and there's the English the Japanese speak. Really, it can get even more complicated than that, because only the English—as only they could—really mastered English. And the only people who really ever understand foreigner's Japanese are other foreigners who went to the same Japanese-language school.

Visitors to Japan get trapped very often because they don't *really* understand their own native language. For instance, I've seen Americans get more than somewhat upset with those girls who sit by the front doors in Tokyo department stores. They get mad because even though the girls wear big buttons that say "I Speak English," they don't seem to understand a word the visitors are saying. If that ever happens to you, please remember that the buttons say "I *Speak* English"—they do not say "I *Understand* English."

I bring that up because I want you to understand how all the Japanized English that Miranda Kenrick has collected came to be in the first place. It's all the product of those "I Speak English" people, a product that provides some of the best entertainment that the "I Understand English" people will ever find anywhere.

The only thing that might be more hilarious, in fact, would be if some of us "I Speak Japanese" folks started putting up Japanese signs back in Cleveland.

By the way, if some of you foreigners now living in Japan happen to understand exactly what the Japanese meant when they put together some of the gems in Miranda Kenrick's charming book, you really should consider going home—tomorrow at the latest. Those who don't might retaliate with humor, like the foreigner who replied to "Is that 'L' as in Rome?" with "No, it's 'R' as in London."

But if you do decide to go home, take this little book with you. Nobody's going to believe you if they don't see it in print.

DON MALONEY

New York

Acknowledgments

GRATEFUL ACKNOWLEDGMENT is made to the *Tokyo Weekender,* which published the series of articles on which this book is based.

Many friends and acquaintances have contributed to the book. Strangers, too, having read the stories in the *Weekender,* have sent me their favorite examples of Japanized English. There are too many to name individually, but I should like to thank in particular Anthony Willoughby, for his help; Barbara Knode and Walter Nichols, who lent me their own archives; Don Maloney, for his kindness in writing the Foreword; and Corky Alexander, editor and publisher of the *Tokyo Weekender.*

The illustrations appearing on page 16 and various other examples of interesting usages of English are reproduced from the section entitled "English as she is Japped," in: *Things Japanese,* by Basil Hall Chamberlain, reprinted as *Japanese Things,* © 1971, by Charles E. Tuttle Co., Inc.

The author would also like to express her indebtedness to the many people, published materials, and numerous examples of printed matter that helped to contribute to and make possible this book.

— 1 —
Photographer Executed

I HAVE LIVED in Tokyo all of my life, and have been amassing "howlers" for most of it. Fortunately for me, Japan is a country rich in examples, and the stunning errors that find their way into print provide constant and continuing entertainment.

Collecting "correctible" English is not a new hobby for Japanophiles. At the turn of the century, eminent British scholar, professor, and writer Basil Hall Chamberlain wrote *Things Japanese*, a glimpse into a new world, one which was then only recently opened to foreign trade and visitors. Chamberlain's introduction to Japan ranges from "Art" and "Abacus" through "History" and "Harakiri" to "Wood Engraving" and "Women." Tucked into the book is a chapter called "English as she is Japped," containing riveting examples of the written English that surrounded him in his life in Japan.

Stationery shops, for instance, offered "hand panting post cards," while clothes could be bought from a "Tailor Native Gountry" or a "Draper, Milliner, and Ladies Outfatter."

I wonder what confidence a doctor could have inspired when he proclaimed himself a "Specialist for the Decease of Children." Or a studio that offered "Photograper Executed."

Cosmetic counters are said to have displayed "Best Perfuming Water Anti Flea," while egg shops sold "extract of fowl" and dairies proudly paraded "pest milk." It was also possible, apparently, to buy not only "fresh laid eggs," but "fresh laid milk" too!

Who could have resisted these next choice items?

Fire shovels advertised themselves thus:

TRADE **K** MARK

*Showvels Scoops and Spades whi-
ch are exhibited of the above trade mark is very cheap in the pi-
ce and it is bonueniemt bor Use.
There is no neceity exklain ally aek-
norulebqe by thebll customers.*

Chamberlain found a beer bottle with a label making
these modest claims:

TRADE MARK

ル ー ビ ジ フ

FUJI BEER

The efficacy of this Beer is to
give the health and especially
the strength for Stomach.
The flovoûr is so sweet
and simple that not
injure for much
drink.

Just think of all the people whose lives must have
been brightened by such promises, and who merrily

drank themselves into oblivion, feeling that they were under the equivalent of doctor's orders.

As for "Fragrant Kozan Wine," its propaganda declared:

> If health be not steady, heart is not active. Were heart active, the deeds must be done. Among the means to preserve health, the best way is to take in Kozan wine which is sold by us, because it is to assist digestion and increase blood. Those who want the steady health should drink Kozan wine. This wine is agreeable even to the females and children who can not drink any spirit because it is sweet. On other words, this pleases mouth and therefore, it is very convenient medicine for nourishing.

A guidebook of Chamberlain's day listed hotels that grandly accommodated the "cessation of travellers." A hotel in Kyoto, Japan's ancient capital and showplace of temples and shrines, posted this stern sign:

NOTICE TO THE DEALERS

On the dinning-time nobody shall be enter to the dinning-room, and drowing-room without the guests' allow. Any dealer shall be honestly his trade, of course the sold one shall be prepare to make up the safe package.

The flow of extraordinary English has continued to proliferate in Japan ever since those early days, and shows little sign of abating. Several years ago, an F. C. Brown of San Francisco shared the following in a letter to the editor of the *Far Eastern Economic Review*. The traffic instructions were, he said, copied verbatim from a sign in a 1930s Japanese police station.

1. At the rise of the hand policeman, stop rapidly.
2. Do not pass him by or otherwise disrespect him.
3. When a passenger of the foot hove in view, tootle the horn; trumpet at him melodiously at first, but if he still obstacles your passage tootle him with vigor and express by word of mouth warning, *"Hi, Hi."*

4. Beware of the wandering hourse that he shall not take fright as you pass him by. Do not explode the exhause box at him. Go soothingly by.
5. Give great space to the festive dog that shall sport in the roadway.
6. Avoid entanglement of dog with wheel spokes.
7. Go soothingly on the grease road as there lurks the skid demon.
8. Press the brake of the foot as you roll around corner to save collapse and tie up.

In those prewar days there were already some English-language daily newspapers in several cities in Japan. Nagasaki, the major port city in southern

Japan, had one, for example. Way back in the sixteenth century, it was the first port into which foreigners had gained a toehold in establishing a trading post, so it was regarded as more cosmopolitan than other cities. (It also provided the setting for Puccini's much loved romantic opera, *Madame Butterfly*.) The papers were painstakingly modeled on respected overseas journals, even copying such features as society columns. But sometimes these things went a little awry. Once a journalist solemnly noted, "The wedding was consummated in the garden of the American Consul's home in the presence of more than a hundred distinguished guests."

DURING THE Occupation years of 1945–52, the Allied forces established bases in many locations all over Japan. Young Japanese people yearned to speak English. They studied at school and applied themselves to memorizing phrases to try out—with lots of giggles—on the new population of Westerners on Japanese streets. Pidgin English became the normal method of communication between housewives and maids, office principals and staff, GI Joes and Tokyo Roses. And inevitably, weird signs in the English language mushroomed.

A bakery declared itself the "biggest loafer in town." A dairy offered "fresh milk squeezed daily from female oxen." A peddler dazzled his customers with his "guaranteed Pure Gold Fish."

A dressmaker announced, "Ladies have fits upstairs." Another proffered "dresses for Ladies and Gentlemen," while a third promised "fur coats made for ladies from their own skins."

Come in and have your thing engraved.

Timid folk steered clear of the Ginza shop that displayed the sign, "Come in and have your thing engraved," while this sign in the toilet of a Tokyo bar produced loud guffaws: "To stop drip, turn cock to right."

You would have been justified in wondering if a diabolically clever someone, somewhere, was devoting his life to the production of these signs. One might even have thought that the authorities were in on the act. For example, the police circulated this ambiguous description of a suspect: "His face was well symetrical and features were few." Probably the suspect was non-Japanese. We're told often enough that Westerners all look alike. . . .

The legal profession was no better. A defendant with a legal problem "made a suitcase to the Tokyo court."

Nor were religious sensibilities entirely safe. This was a description of the birth of Buddha: "The princess had been caught by a fit of giving birth to a child. By a sudden no sooner had dazzling beams got in and shone her than a perfect pretty boy got born with cheerful cry."

And this was from a letter from a Christian complaining about a Buddhist priest: "We indignated on it long time. What? Buddhist should do. I encourage Buddhists to practice their what they preach."

A Christian minister wrote a tract about prewar and wartime suppression of Christianity in Japan. It was enthusiastically reviewed by a Japanese, who began: "Let us intoxicate by unequalled excellent description to all ages written by author. Let us enjoy with the skillful passages of ironical expression described all over the sentences written by author who is hiding his unopressible feeling of a angry at the bottom of his breast."

The faithful encountered other unexpected hazards. A local staff reporter said of an outdoor public sermon preached by the founder of one of the new Messianic religions: "People were literally jammed in the reduced area of the garden, leaving no elbow room for them, not to speak of some spaces for their breath-taking."

Nevertheless, the most famous, most repeated

story of all Occupation "howlers" must be the one that concerns Douglas MacArthur—known to some as "Dagrass MacArser"—when his name was being bandied around as a possible candidate for the presidency of the United States.

To demonstrate their feelings, supporters raised an enormous banner in downtown Tokyo. It flaunted these immortal words, "WE PLAY FOR MACARTHUR'S ERECTION."

— 3 —
Cars Will Not Have Intercourse on This Bridge

SINCE SO MANY Westerners drove cars around Japan after the war, the Japanese authorities took it upon themselves to clarify, in English, the rules of the road. What dictionaries could they possibly have consulted to come up with some of their signs?

For example, in 1948 a local Tokyo police department issued this traffic bulletin: "When meeting an advancing person tootle your horn vigorously and he will disappear." Among other postwar signs on the road were:

Vertical Parking Only.
Have Many Accidents Here.
Try Bigger and Bigger but keep More and More Slowly.
Let's Reduce Noise by Ourselves.
Cars will not have Intercourse on this Bridge.

Over the years, over the decades, official Japanese departments have maintained their outpouring in the English language. In the 1970s the Tax Office had this to say to certain folk, tardy in their payments:

Dear Tax Payer: On the 31st October we sent you a reference from and begged you to send back it till the 10th November. But we have not received your answer up to the present day the 25th November. We send you same reference form once more and beg you to accomplish and send back it to us as soon as possible. Thank you for your comprehension.

* * *

Not to be outdone, another official department prepared its "requesting for Payment of Electric Charges: We have not as yet enjoyed the happiness of being in receipt of the above electric charges billed to you and wish to dare remind you of the whole payment period coming near to its close. We hope, and should appreciate if, you would cooperate for the smooth operation of our business by kindly taking the trouble of bringing this card to, and paying the bill direct at, our office mentioned below not later than the coming August 25th."

The ending is polite, but firm: "We wish to call it to your kind attention that we should be very sorry if, by your failing to pay the bill by the above-mentioned date, we were obliged to discontinue servicing you with our electricity in accordance with the provision of our 'Rules and Rates for Electric Service.'"

One nuisance necessitated by being a foreign resident in Japan is having to register your presence with the authorities, having to carry an "alien registration" card at all times—woe betide you if you're caught without it—and having to apply for permission to reenter Japan each time you leave the country.

As for permission to live here, . . . but no, I won't go into that, except to say that for residents on six-month or one-year visas, necessary visits to the Immigration Office seem to come around very often. Nor were the previous Offices ever in convenient parts of town.

In the mid-1980s, however, the Immigration Office finally prepared to move to Otemachi, smack in the business area of downtown Tokyo. Full directions to reach the new facilities were posted in the building that was being vacated. Travel by public transportation was advised. "Do not use parking lot as we expect a great deal of dustle," concluded the notice.

On the subject of immigration, the Alien Registration Law spells out Ward Office registration requirements: "Those who become aliens, while in Japan, by birth or any other reasons" must register within 30 days. How, I wonder, would one set about *becoming* an alien?

*   *   *

The Rotary Club of Japan once showed its concern

in sending out this circular: "Ladies Day. This is too late a notice to tell you that this meeting has been made a Ladies Day in hope to have your ladies hear about the recent explosion in the Marunouchi area, killing 8 and injuring 300 passers-by. Who and why will be analyzed by a *Mainichi* man in the local section." (The *Mainichi* is a daily newspaper, just in case you're wondering what sort of man this might be.)

In Japan we are often told—and, it would seem, no wonder!—to beware of things. "Beware of flashing toilet," for instance. Or "beware of clothes that run," as the sign in the laundromat warns.

This, in a recording studio, doesn't actually say "beware," but it sounds like an admonition, nevertheless. A plaque attached to a machine cautions, "Disk playing. Amprifire."

A neighborhood sign rules, "It is forbidden your

dog exclement." The obedient nervously carry small spades and bags as they walk their dogs. Evidence is swiftly scooped up as they go, so you'd never know the dogs had been around.

Within an apartment building is the injunction, "No smoking while walking." Is the day approaching when we are required not to talk, lick ice cream cones, or chew gum as we walk?

Two notices arrive, on separate occasions, from the water department. One says in English, "We'll be a water supply works near your home. We give a person trouble to noise the while please acknowledge."

The other, thrust in our letterbox, is in Japanese, with these scrawled words in English: "Tomorrow, from midnight to 12 noon, you will receive dirty water."

— 33 —

Well, twelve hours is a long time to be receiving dirty water, so it's nice to be warned. But someone once told me of the time when notices were plastered all over the elevator in her apartment building. They were in red ink and looked so important that she enlisted the aid of a Japanese friend for a translation. Apparently, she was told, the electric power was to be suspended the next day for one minute, and the residents' indulgence was begged.

"One minute?" she echoed incredulously.

"One minute," confirmed her Japanese friend.

A notice in an apartment garage begins: "We are reported that a car in our parking lot was damaged by naughty person. In order to prevent the above, we management, strengthen our patrol in that area. We would be much appreciated for your cooperation as to reporting to us whenever you see a person doing the act."

The gas company is also guilty of bloopers. When we investigated the installation of a gas heater with a fan to help warm our winters, the estimate gave a price for "gas fun for entrance holl." Ah well, perhaps those extra degrees of warmth will indeed make us inclined to have fun during the winter.

— 4 —
Are You Haunted by Horribles?

WHEN IT COMES TO health, you want—indeed, you *need*—genuine understanding with your physician. Yes, there are European and American doctors practicing in Japan. Yes, there are Japanese doctors who have trained overseas and whose English is complete. However, there are also some Japanese doctors whose English is not *quite* as complete.

Once upon a long time ago, a Japanese doctor gave a patient a bottle of Mercotin tablets. His prescription was: "1 tablet 3 times a day until passing away. For prevention of nocturnal cough, 1 tablet more at bed time."

Actually, things haven't changed much since then. Quite recently, before a medical overhaul, I received these instructions from a doctor: "Please one tablet of gall fluoroscopy helpers by 3 p.m. of the previous day to make sure nothing happens and then take the rest at 5 minutes interval from 9 p.m. Diarrhoea is no problem, but if this caused measles please do not take any more and tell so at the counter."

— Dosage —

Adults: 1 tablet 3 times a day until passing away. For prevention of nocturnal cough, 1 tablet more at bed time.

Medical forms in Japan do not stand on ceremony. Instead they ask such personal questions as:

Are you haunted by horribles?

Do you ever run after your nose?

Does your nose choke?

Does your head or face or shoulder ever limp?

Has any part of your body suddenly grown uncontrollable?

Do you have heart thrills?

Do you have hot fit?

Do you have shiver of fingers?

Do you feel as if there were two when there is only one?

Are more than half your teeth off?

Do you ever have a drilling pain in your stomach?

Do your sholders or scruff of the neck grow stiff?

Do you always have trouble with your body?

Have you been influenced by Atom bomb?

Did your doctor tell you you have abnormal body?

Have you been put into a mental hospital?

Do you readily become orderless unless you are strained?

To encourage people to be responsible for their own health, a company launched a gadget for taking one's own blood pressure. The advertisement advises: "You can know an anxious blood pressure precisely by yourself. Especially minimal blood pressure should be always in your grasp for your happy life."

Another advertisement recommends, "to avoid the morning after, take oyster extract before drinking alcohol." Oyster extract, apparently, is good for men "in case be weak, or be anxious diabetes, the liver, or heart disease." Women, it says, need oyster extract "in case unseasonal monthly period, be cold natured, or get roughened."

The blurb with a self-massaging machine states: "Many people feel stiffness or ache on their back or neck. They cannot, however, rub or beat freely by themselves. With this, you can make massage or finger pressure cure lightly."

A pamphlet on first aid says: "A convulsive fit does not directly endanger patient's life. So there is no need to panic. It will end spontaneously while you are watching him.

"For epilepsy wrap chopstick in cloth and put it between his upper and lower teeth to prevent him from biting his tongue. P.S. Handkerchief can be used instead of chopstick.

"To rouse unconscious patients apply vinegar, perfume, or ammonia fumes to his nose, dash water on his face, call his name loudly or rap him on hand or foot."

To check the temperature of hot-water bottles,

— 5 —
Do Not Enter Bath with Soap Bubbling Body

To USE THE facilities of an international hotel in Japan is to receive superior service, attentiveness, and pampering. You will also be bombarded with signs in English. Restaurants have menus in English, beauty parlors and barbers have price lists in English, the rooms themselves are chock-full of useful information in English.

One hotel offers "an abbreviated but true tea ceremony—for even quite a stranger a trial will serve you somewhat appreciable of inherent implication of the traditional art of life—with a touch of modern fesability—making you realize, but for the grace of refined etiquette and formality, spirit hardly goes much far in life."

Another hotel's restaurant says "unglazed tile, goatskin seat coverings, copper medallions and light softly falling from the ceiling contribute to an excellent atmosphere for grilling meat."

It may be that all you want is to sit quietly over a drink, but for some coffee shops atmosphere is crucial. One invites you to "enjoy snacks and coffee in a light airy room. Sunlight filters through young trees that change with the seasons—young buds in spring, green leaves in summer, red in autumn, bare in winter."

Some signs from yesteryear are true classics, remembered and quoted to this day. A Tokyo hotel bar once offered "special cocktails for ladies with nuts." Printed on another hotel's restaurant menu was, "All vegetables served in this restaurant are washed in water passed by our head chef."

"MAKE FACIAL CUT" was the shorthand message in large letters across the window of a beauty shop in a Tokyo hotel. Another hotel's "hair dressing menu" offered "for party," "for new style," "for relaxation," "for maintenance of hair style," "for grooming," and "for busy men."

A welcome note from a hotel says, "It's a all means the same things to have you our guests."

Welcome and service fall over each other in this story. An Australian man leaves his camera case on a hotel counter while he makes a phone call. When he returns, the camera bag has vanished. Consternation! Then a bell boy trots over and solemnly hands him a handwritten note: "Dear Sir. Your room is in your camera case."

A door in a hotel is marked "Stuff Only." A long-ago swing door said "Push" on one side and "Ouch" on the other. Another door of that era said "Hit" on one side and "Drag" on the other. How dull, how ordinary it is nowadays, just to "push" and "pull."

A message by the telephone in a hotel room reads, "Glittering night view and a golden drink. Dial 2 for your gorgeous time." How eagerly and how frequently 2 must have been dialed!

Hotel bathrooms have their ambiguities too. One has these labels above the faucets: "Volume on," "Squelch," and "Please dial to shut whenever you want to."

The message on a hand-drying machine in a hotel rest room says, "Put your wet hands into below pocket. Fully automatic air blow gives you an instant speedy dry up."

Many a sign in English, in many a hotel, is there to discourage—or outright forbid—you from indulging in certain activities. Other signs apologize for inconveniencing you.

Here are a few that have, at one time or another, been displayed in one Japanese hotel or another:

The elevator is fixed for the next day. During that time we regret you will be unbearable.

Use this elevator. Fright elevator in repair.

Depositing the room key into another person is prohibited.

Swindlers dangling with guests around our hotel at night have no relations with us. Beware and do not be cheated by their skillful enticements.

Kindly do not make noise for some people prefer to sleep.

No smoking in bed and other disgusting behaviors.

Is forbidden to steal hotel towels please. If you are not person to do such thing please not to read this notis.

Do not put towel and soup in bath.

Do not hang wet clothes on lump shades.

One hotel official wrote to a guest: "I was informed from our Security Staff today regarding the reception room of swimming pool, of this room you are using to store the stuff. He says 'there are many vacant beer cans and cigarette butts scattered around there and it is possible to cause fire.' Please put much intention and keep your eye on this room."

A youth hostel in Japan has this sign: "To our guests under construction." Another asks for "register of names lodging parson," "lodging birth," and "the other day lodging land." Which probably (but not certainly) means, quite simply, name, date of birth, and where did you spend last night?

Day begins at 6:30 in some hostels with "getting up and cleaning a poom." You're thrown out at 10:00 for "any person except those especially permitted can no tremain."

Emergency instructions in Japanese hotels include this one in the garage of a Tokyo hotel: "Provided

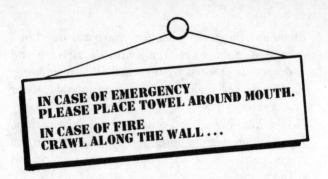

IN CASE OF EMERGENCY
PLEASE PLACE TOWEL AROUND MOUTH.

IN CASE OF FIRE
CRAWL ALONG THE WALL ...

at this room with carbon dioxide fire extinguishing system. Alarm by voice is broadcasted before discharging CO_2 gas. Take shelter to outside immediately."

Precautions against fires include, "In case of emergency please place towel around mouth." (Could this be to ensure a silent exit?)

A country hotel writes, "Dear Our Guests: Every possible effort is being made to prevent a fire and other disastrous occurances." The notice goes on to require guests, in case of fire, to "crawl along the wall. Do not get back to your room again for searching your valuables, etc. after flet to the safety place."

In another hotel a flashlight, attached to the wall in a corridor, has this plaque under it: "Flush light. Just pull down and let's go."

＊　　＊　　＊

Until modern times, when home bathrooms became more general, the usual practice was for people to go out to communal bathhouses. Going to the bath was an evening outing, a highlight at the end of day, as jolly as going to a pub or a club in other countries. Public baths still exist today. In the cities men and women usually have separate rooms, and in the resorts the sexes are often separated too, but still in some hot-spring districts huge public baths accommodate men, women, and children all together.

Japanese bathing practice is the same everywhere: to wash and rinse outside the bathtub, to be clean before getting into the water to soak, and to leave the hot water unsullied for the next bather. Naive foreigners have sometimes caused horror by emptying bathtubs after use. This led the proprietor of a ski resort lodge to put up a notice that said, "Foreigners are requested not to pull cock in Japanese bath."

In the mid-1960s an Englishwoman stayed in a traditional Japanese inn in Kyoto, city of traditions. A hotel maid entered her room, knelt, bowed, and offered an intriguing document. It gave written instructions in English on how to use the Japanese bath. Alas, the maid smartly whipped the paper away, allowing time for just one brief reading. But even without the chance to copy or memorize it, one phrase registered, never to be forgotten: "Do not enter bath with soap bubbling body."

— 6 —
Do Not Throw Foreign Bodies in the Toilet

FOR MANY YEARS after the Occupation of Japan ended, America retained control of Okinawa, a chain of islands to the south of the four main islands of Japan. During that time, this sign greeted visitors at the airport in Naha, the capital city: "Welcome. You have just arrived in an area which was formerly affected by malaria. This disease has been eradicated after a long and costly campaign. But a single person carrying malaria parasites in his blood may infect local mosquitoes and contribute to a malaria epidemic."

While Okinawa was protecting its local mosquitoes, Tokyo was doing its bit for foreigners. Through the 1960s, signs in the rest rooms at Haneda Airport, then the main air entrance to Japan, commanded, "Do not throw foreign bodies in the toilet."

As the volume of air traffic and the size of the aircraft outgrew Haneda, it was clear that a new international airport was needed to serve Tokyo. The authorities chose Narita, some 60 kilometers distant in Chiba Prefecture, for the New Tokyo International Airport. Chiba farmers and residents, who resented the interruption of their lives and the loss of their land, demonstrated vigorously against the development. For years they even managed to prevent its opening.

But the authorities eventually won, and the location of the airport has made an enormous difference to Tokyo's visitors and residents—for the long journey to and from Narita can be the most tedious part of any international trip.

New rail and bus services were inaugurated to carry passengers to and from the airport. And with the new services, a slew of literature appeared. At the Skyliner train station was this sign: "If you want to take non-smoking car, please offer to sell ticketer."

Meanwhile, the Tokyo City Air Terminal sported this ambiguous sign: "You are not allowed to smoke three rows from foremost to all buses."

Not to be outdone, the airport limousine service (actually a bus service) put out a pamphlet that said, "We appreciate your cooperation for the prevention of bus jack." It went on: "Put your baggage in the belly of the bus. You can enjoy sweet accommodations and enough space and reclining seat. Please make yourself at home at your favourite angle." And on: "We can carry pets by Limousine, but you should hold them in a pen or a cage with yourself."

In the seat pockets were "clean packs" and "emergency cards." The clean pack, said the helpful explanation, was to be used "if you feel sick or you can do it as a trash bag." The emergency card said: "Please show the driver a Red Card in case of sudden illness and a Blue Card when you wish to use a rest room urgently. He will take care of you in accordance with the situations."

Finally, this sign stood before an out-of-order escalator at Narita Airport: "An escalator avobe this notice is under repair hopeing to be savoured with yours use of northern escalator or elevator."

Meanwhile, there have long been baffling signs at train stations around Japan. In the late 1950s this one hung at Hamamatsucho station in Tokyo, which was the nearest city train station to the port where you boarded a ship for the outlying islands. "Change train here into ship for Izu Islands," said the sign. Just one flick of your magic wand should do it.

One railway station had a "waiting room for parties," while another required the public to "wait until the door is open before passing through. Passengers will line up in rows of two at times of conjection." Another station reminded us that "flowers and fish are here to be loved."

The old resort town of Karuizawa, deep in the mountains, has long been a summer retreat for foreign residents (who, perhaps, do not know that its name is derived from the Ainu words for "Great Pumice Stone Moor"). Periodically this sign went up at the railway station: "You are prohibited from

Climbing Mt. Asama for it is acting now." Mt. Asama is a live volcano.

A ship, too, had rules and regulations, including, "For safety of life cargo and ship, it is prohibited to bring swords, guns, rifles, and other inflammables and explosives into cabin without permission if you have such things with you. Please apply to information. Crew will keep them as long as you are among passengers."

A local ferry boat once advertised that it had a "first class lady toilet." Another's emergency procedures included these instructions: "In an emergency whistle and motor siren 7 or more staccato blows will be sounded followed by 1 long blow. Passengers will assemble on upper decks in calm. Attention to passengers when using Chuter to get to Life Raft. Sit down with your legs stretched forward in a natural manner. You will be down in a few seconds so feel easy and get sliding with your face turned up. Once down do not try to stand up in a hurry, get up only after sliding is well over."

— 7 —
Picture Quest Pot

TRAVELING AND "see-sighting" anywhere in Japan has always multiplied the chances of stumbling over hilarious signs in English. Once, for example, during the 1950s, an observation place on a mountain road had a sign in English. It meant to say—surely it meant to say—"picturesque spot." Instead, however, it identified itself as a "picture quest pot."

Often, it's not necessary to go far from Tokyo to find such signs. Nikko, for example, is encompassable in a day. It's a town of temples and shrines—altogether a most extravagant display of religious architecture—made famous as the burial place of Tokugawa Ieyasu, the first Japanese shogun. Above Nikko in the mountains is Lake Chūzenji, which is surrounded by hotels and cottages suitable for long summer retreats. Nikko is also famous for its botanical garden, and between 1948 and 1955 this sign was posted at its entrance: "No picnicking, no botanizing and no uproaring in these gardens."

A sign at a mountainside rest area near Nikko warns people against making eye contact with wild monkeys, lest the animals feel threatened and attack. At least, that's what it said in Japanese. In English, the warning translated to "Do not open your face to monkeys."

Hakone isn't very far away, either, and as well as the glories of the lakes and a view across to Mt. Fuji, the area boasts a national park. Conscious of its potential for tourist development, the authorities have prepared a tourist map with delightful English descriptions of the special sights to be visited. One is a "place noted for suicide (hanging and poison taking suicide)." Shoot yourself and you'd be an absolute idiot!

Nara, one of Japan's ancient capitals, houses Hōryūji, the oldest temple in Japan and one of the world's oldest wooden structures. Replete with temples and gardens, it is also famous for its park, in which deer roam free. At the end of the 1960s, a prominent notice greeted visitors thus:

Elsewhere, another park posted this injunction: "Please do not enter. This is a park for some old ladies."

Written instructions in public places range from "fire escaper" and "do not throw" to such signs as these in public rest rooms:

- VISITORS ARE ASKED TO LEAVE THE TOILETS IN A CLEAN CONDITION.

- AN INCINERATOR IS PROVIDED BEHIND THE ENTRANCE DOOR.

- PLEASE USE YOUR FOOT TO HANDLE THE COCK.

- PLEASE PUSH DRAIN BUTTON AFTER USE AND THROW IN DUST CAN WITHOUT TOILET PAPER.

Subterranean caves in Okinawa once commanded: "No smoking, no photographing. Stalactites and stalagmites grow one millimeter every 3 years. Please do not touch and hands off them. Here is the middle pleace. Have a nice cave tour."

To this day, signs around Japan are of never-ending interest. "Please walk on the paved carpet," for one. "Let's have a great protection for the old fragile cultural assets," for another.

A museum—not an "antic museum," although there are such places—requires visitors to "refrain from taking photographs and reproducing." But you wouldn't *think* of doing so, would you?

Osaka, Japan's third largest city, frequently hosts trade fairs. At a recent international trade exhibition, a sign in front of a collection of European drawings claimed they were there to promote "cultural exchange and trade friction."

In 1970, attention focused on Osaka when it hosted a World Exposition. This dire warning was posted around the fair grounds at Expo '70:

WARNING! Gentlemen!

Please do not carry your wallets in rear pocket for your backside is easily attacked.

Five years later, special attractions at the Ocean Expo in Okinawa included "bug pipes" from the U.K. and a "string quarter" from Australia.

A news release said: "*Gomennasai*. On Weekly News Release No. 13, item (6) says 'Mosquito Class Yacht Race'. This was our amateurish and poor knowledge mistake. Please correct to 'Moth Class Yacht Ract'. Thank you."

As Expo drew to a close, a hotel offered a "*sayonara* plan," and circularized this notice: "On the 18th January 1976 the Ocean Exposition in Okinawa do-coming to the final goal. Which is succeeded in fluentry with happiness. For your great efforts during the terms, we should have the chance to contact in some kind of the planning. Up to this moment we want to you advise and greeding with under plan-

ning. Before you leaving Okinawa, please stand-by
and enjoy yourself."

*   *   *

Beppu is a holiday town on the southernmost island
of Kyushu. Its attraction? Hot water. Or, more precisely, healing medicinal waters, with mud pools
(known as Hells), and hot sands into which people
are buried to their necks and steamed back to vita-
lity and health. It also once boasted a children's
"Sportsland" in an amuseument center. This contained a "lovely train driven by tame monkey" and
a "magic house where anyone will be quite surprised
and utter 'S.O.S.' 100 percent thrill."

Near the Sportsland was an electric science museum where "the wonders of electricity are displayed
for children to be easily digested."

CHILDREN'S SPORTSLAND

MAGIC HOUSE WHERE ANYONE WILL BE QUITE
SURPRISED AND UTTER "S.O.S."
100 PERCENT THRILL.

ELECTRIC SCIENCE MUSEUM

THE WONDERS OF ELECTRICITY ARE DISPLAYED
FOR CHILDREN TO BE EASILY DIGESTED.

Even if you aren't much of a traveler, tourist literature is always worth studying. The extravagance of
some claims makes you question the reality, but
there's always entertainment in the reading. One
pamphlet says: "Beautiful Nagara River, verdur-
ous Mt. Kinka, scenic Gifu Castle and noted cormorants fishing on the River Nagara which are
symbolic off he good old tradition of Japan, possess
the optimum surroundings to have enough of the
Japanese emotion. The resort hotels standing on
both sides of the Nagara River offer the visitors a
relaxing atmosphere to enjoy the romantic mood
of the spa to their hear hearts content."

Although an industrial city, Gifu is renowned
for the tradition of cormorant fishing, where the birds
are trained to catch fish. In spectacular pageants
which highlight the summer evenings, master train-
ers on river boats hold cormorants on rope leashes

that they pay out as the birds take to the water. When a cormorant catches a fish the trainer pulls him back on board the boat and takes it from his beak. We are told in a helpful leaflet that "the birds cannot swallow the fish because their long necks are tied on with string."

Skimming through a brochure praising the scenic beauty of the island of Shikoku, I see this remarkable sentence: "The simple-minded inhabitants are bright as larks and are blessed with good health."

Another brochure entitled "The Origin of Shichi-mi Red Pepper" lauds the beauties of Kyoto's Kiyomizu Temple, one of the loveliest temples in a city known for total loveliness. The approach to it is up a steep hill, affectionately known as Teapot Lane. Small, old-fashioned shops line Teapot Lane. One of these is a family business selling, of all things, red pepper. The brochure that comes with the pepper says: "The house of Shichi-mi, close to the famous Kiyomizu Temple, was founded almost three hundred years ago and nowadays this Shichi-mi Family is so famous that everyone knows the existence of this house. It is the origin of this house that the red pepper was given persons to encourage who meditated under the fall named Otowa of Kiyomizu Temple by being struck themselves by the water fall at that time. After this red pepper was improved soon by adding the sweet-smelling and tasty substances, it was named Shichi-mi. This was the first time to sell whole in Japan and this was done by my ancestor."

Picture, if you will, naked men braced against the icy crash of a waterfall. And red pepper to the rescue—"to encourage who meditated!"

A hotel invites you to:

Return to nature only three hour ride away from Tokyo!
In snowy hills hares and foxes hop around and in streams trouts and chars swim about. Also you will enjoy the glare of sun beams and fresh ozone.
Down at the foot of the 4200 feet over sea-leveled hotel, there are factories of cameras, watches, and music boxes.

Mashiko is a favorite destination in Japan. It is the home of folkcraft pottery, forever associated with potter Shōji Hamada (designated a Living National Treasure), who dedicated his life to preserving and passing on traditional pottery techniques.

A long-ago leaflet of the district is called a "Guid of a Haniwa (clay idol)" and says:

About 1700 years ago, when the Mikoto of Yamato-hiko was buried, . . . his perple were buried around his grave just as they alived. It must be beyond description imaginable their miserable voices which they are crying day and night as long as they lived. It seems the custom of the immolation of ons self on the death of one's lord has populared since long ago. . . . Then the idea was appointed . . . to make men and horsed with earth instead of man who die with his lord. . . . And the business which they make men horses and chinaware with earth was began. . . . This thing was made by which is the materiad for Mashiko yaki. . . . We have been studied for many years and now we could make a thing as never sam clour and same form."

Meanwhile, a small Shinto shrine in the heart of Tokyo has this sign: "The God enshrined in this Toriizaka Inari accords happiness and worldly treasures to all the people who blieves in The God and protects people from evils and ill omens unbelievable capacity indeed. If you believe in this God it is said that when you travel by plane or by car your safety is assured and you will ascape from harm disaster or fatal accidents. Because of this Toriizaka Inari is also called Aviation Inari."

＊　　　＊　　　＊

While the British have their weather, the Japanese have their seasons. In addition to the usual four, they have several others. There is the "rainy season," which divides spring and summer; and the "typhoon season," which divides summer and autumn. Then there's the "cherry blossom season," when large parties of people eat, drink, and get very drunk under the cherry trees; and the "leaf-viewing

season" in autumn, when the same people do more or less the same thing under the maple trees.

During the rainy season, it is hot, humid, and very wet for several weeks, and you have your work cut out battling the encroaching mildew. There are compensations, however. A pamphlet lauds the hydrangea, a flower that "appeals its lovely charm in rain and gives us heartwarming refreshment during groomy weather in Japan."

The article goes on to say: "Originally born and raised in Japan, this neat flower is very popular for headges and gardens. . . . In colors of blue, pink, and purple, round shaped Hydrangea looks like a handball. When they are gathered and in full bloom, they will catch your eyes and never let them go."

— 8 —
Mice Meat Pies, Salad Bowels, and Poison

FLING THE NET wide and haul in your Japanized English. Today's catch could include such phrases as "all ladies are half price." This is the 1987 advertisement of a Tokyo bar.

But first let's spin back through time to the days when almost everything written in English guaranteed a giggle.

Decades ago there was an enticing sign on a road in Kansai. It said:

> WEL COME TO
> JAPAN THE SEA
> MEN YOU GENTL-
> MEN DROP IN THE
> BAR KING AT GIRST:
> LADIES ARE READY
> *In boxes and stands*

Among the many things it *might* mean is that ladies could be found in booths and stand-up bars, eager to entertain newly arrived sailors.

In more recent years, bars have posted such signs as "Girls speak English, French, German, and Spanish. This is too good an opportunity for foreigners."

The girls within might be singers, rendering such favorites as "Moon Liver," while the bar might well offer a "bottle yourself keeping system."

One recent summer a couple of American teenagers worked as "cocktail servers" in a Tokyo restaurant. When they first applied, they were handed four typed pages of instructions in English for their "very important job having responsibility to sell the drinks." The document pointed out that "naturally the more expensive drinks taste the better, and you are supposed to recommend the better ones to the guests." However, the restaurant was also prepared for guests "unable to drink alcoholics."

The girls would be expected to stay alert and, at appropriate moments, offer fresh drinks "for it will be too late if you take orders after it's drunk up caused taking time to make new one at the bar." After all, the restaurant was well aware that "human body requires more and more alcohol when they start drinking. Usually having a drink makes them soonly require another drinks."

The written memo also covered "handling a tray." The requirements would be:

1. Cocktail Servers always walk around with trays in the restaurant.
2. Lift your tray always with one hand unless carring many drinks at once or taking many empty glasses away.
3. High glasses or heavy glasses should be carried closed on your body side on the tray.
4. When you bring Menues, keep them nicely under your one arm.

Another duty would be to "remember the guests as many as possible and try to make them constant comers."

From bars to bakeries, tidbits abound. One bakery's motto is: "We wish all the time to be able to provide you fresh bread and to propose you a joy of eating life with bread. Especially we want to be a host at dinner of your kitchen." Meanwhile, another offers "dogs and croissant petty brunch." There are also "dogs for take out."

A certain cake shop's slogan is: "Sweet Fit. If your curiosity is such, That sets your heart on, Endless adventures, Let it persist, It will rest where, You find, Life that fits you, Then feel the height of luxury, Be chic and cool, A woman serene and sophisticated, with no chip on her shoulder, Living free but not way out, Call her a sweet fit."

Then there are the coffee shops. Start with their names: "Jack, Betty's Friend." "Cry Baby's Egg." "Tasty Crub." "Pee Ka Boo." "Titty Boo." "Le Gland." "Burial." "Hot Staff." "Muck."

If you dare enter, you'll be given a "menew" and then the fun begins.

You could be offered all sorts of drinks. "Flesh juice" or "pain juice" or "ginger whale." There's "hott iced tea" and "the highest black tea," and "profuse dairy drinks." Or "natural gas," "bear," "raw beer," or "fizz and toll drinks." There is also "white hores whiskey" and "badwiser beer" and "wine squash."

"Lice" and "blead" are staples, before you move on to "aspa-rags" soup. There are "humbug" or "catlet sand witches." Or "salad bowels." Or "beak potetos," and "sour crout." "Flying bits" turn out to be chicken, potatoes, and croquettes with salad, while a "smokey roaster" is roast chicken.

You might order "fried fishermen," "chopped children," or "cuban livers." There is always

"hushed beef" or "park," "lamp with bees" (lamb with peas), "rumrack" (rack of lamb), "potted good gulp shrimps" and "crumb chops." Or how do "mice meat pies" appeal to you?

Utterly mysterious are "buttered saucepans," "fried hormones," and "brain special." There are "hot dogs and dessert dogs." Or "eggplant melty cheese, over baked," or "cooked well bean strings."

A Chinese restaurant offers "bean cord lightly rice" and "tea poured rice and seeweed."

There's "died" food. And French restaurants are capable of offering you "poison." Just that. Poison.

To continue along the gastronomic trail requires a certain amount of reading, and I pounce on restaurant advertisements from motives other than sheer greed. Just the other day a popular brunch was advertised in a daily newspaper. It offered, among its many sumptuous courses, "original cordon blew" dishes.

Part of a tempura restaurant's pamphlet says:

"Tempura is shrimp and other tasty deep sea goodies deep fried in oil before your eyes. Our restaurant has been doing their tempura thing for 70 years."

Sukiyaki is a popular Japanese dish of thin slices of simmered meat and vegetables served in a soup into which a raw egg is added. One sukiyaki restaurant provides written instructions for dealing with the raw egg. The instructions conclude with, "If the raw egg routine is inconvenient to you, then please skip it."

There's a steak house in Tokyo that "fosters authentic beef with deep affection. . . . Beef has characteristics and physical property and mind as human fairsex has them. You will never eat the beef with the same taste as you are now eating forever."

Meanwhile, a teppanyaki steak restaurant which you might prefer to avoid says that its food is prepared "before your cooked right eyes."

A local French restaurant describes itself thus: "The interior is fully decorated with marvellous marble, and enchanted with the coiling light decorated with a mass of wine glassed glittering alike a gorgeous chandelier. Wines are superb all imported from original places in European countries sealed with the Age."

A local Indian restaurant proudly proclaims: "As spices are said flavor not only emphasize taste and smell but also they are efficacious. Basis of spices Indian foods are exactly the source of health. Unconsciously healthy body will be."

A local Swiss restaurant's pamphlet tells us that it is a "chain chop" and furthermore has a "Pub London very nice London style." Says the pamphlet, "You will have dinner joyfully in the Alpen mood . . . we serve you friendly just like our real family."

It goes on to say that "food is the same as a state of language distribution . . . but the most famous cuisine is Fondue. We believe you relish real taste."

As for the wine: "Europeans are without missing wine on their tables which is water in the life. We have House wine and of course very nice Swiss wine. The great speciality in a dream." On it goes: "The great peaceful nature Look like that peace. . . . The modern civilization lost us adventures, spirits, or elasticity, but we could improve our mind completely by the great natural atmosphere of the Alps. And also a clean peaceful view of valley, plain, river and lake in the country will help our improvement. . . . The Alps gillters in the snow can be seen in the distance. We always think that we would like to care of their hearts who live in such a beautiful country."

The point of all this philosophy, incidentally, is simply to explain the restaurant's "way of thinking about service."

— 9 —
Queer Aid Chocolate, Calpis, and Creap

WHEN IT COMES TO food and drink, it's often not just the menus that startle you. Go into a supermarket via its entrance, and before you go out of the "ex-itrance," browse for a while. You're almost certain to find extraordinary claims written on cans or wrappers.

Yakult—that's a drink, by the way—promotes itself with: "Cheer Up With 'Yakult'—'Yakult' is the health drink manufactured with scientifically cultivated micro-organisms which has tremendously beneficial role to the human intestines. Our firm confidence is based on the fact this live bacteria can go through strong acid in the stomach and bile and reach the intestines alive. Drink 'Yakult' every day without skip, then 'Yakult' will be one of your inseparables."

After that, what could possibly surprise you? Not blue cheese labeled "finest moldy cheese," nor cherries called "these cherry sweet," nor tuna fish dubbed "right meet tuna." Not "liver putty." Not "King of Kings" chocolate or candy in band-aid wrappers that say "Hand maid taste. Queer aid choco." Not even "germ bread," "chocolate sand cookies," "tarty gourmet" cookies, nor "Cutey Alice" cake with its message, "Little Alice said, 'A bite of cake may make you little and take you to wonderland.' "

On the supermarket shelves you'll find "cheddar with cralet" which turns out to be cheddar cheese with a strain of claret. There's "salted cad" at the fish counter and "dill pickless" and "arti chokes" with the vegetables.

bon appetit

There's a coffee creamer called "Creap," a fermented milk drink called "Calpis," and a sports drink called "Pocari Sweat."

As for the candy in Japan, one is "Carap," another "Collon." One chocolate proclaims that "each piece fills you with friendly fantasies and romantic reveries." Another wrapper says: "Beautiful things are beyond time. Women's history cease to yearn for beauty."

Another chocolate "gives you the warm feeling of love. Very graceful, sweet and more lovely chocolate make yourself with Cecil." Another has the "delicate taste of brandy soaked apple in the heart."

A "bourbon pure cut" is a "pure and fresh candy for the pure," while another bourbon candy comes in two flavors. The mint one says, "Let's enjoy sports and this refreshing fragrance of mint" and the lemon one says, "Let's enjoy refreshing sports and this intense sourness."

There's ice cream "in a corn" and "mixed ice ream with wiped cream." A chewing gum wrapper says, "Memories of your elegant fragrance."

A box of fruit cookies blathers: "How sweet it is, how alluring it is, how eternally fresh it is, this forbidden fruit. All the sparkling morning, the breeze is gently warm and soft. Remember the sweet memories of childhood. There were fruit trees in the tiny old garden. They filled the air with wonderful smells. Sweet and soft, sweet and soft. On a bright sunny afternoon you can make sweet memories in the orchard with someone nice."

A box of strawberries comes with this wrapping paper: "When you have strawberry, please prefer milk if possible. Adding milk and sugar, mash strawberry enough by spoon, then the Yogurt is made within it. The Yogurt contains plenty of lactic bacteria which acts strongly on sterilizing the other bad bacterium in human intestine. For this reason, he who wishes to live long, use always Yogurt. Fresh strawberry with milk promote further your health."

*   *   *

You're seldom far from a vending machine in any Japanese town. Or village. Or even halfway up Mt. Fuji, for that matter. They just about line some streets, especially those around the train stations. Avert your eyes from the ones filled with pornographic magazines, ignore those filled with bottles of whiskey, and home in instead on those selling canned drinks.

Cans containing iced coffee say on them: "Nice ladies so busy. Whenever she feels blue, she needs to refresh herself with a chic and stylish mood. Now being alive, healthy, beauty and sexy ladies, have a city drink just for you, mac fresh coffee."

A lemon-flavored drink says on its tin: "Good morning, dear lemons. How juicy you look today."

An apple tea is "very dandy and charming beverage. Its richness and fresh flavor of apple will bring us to the world of fantasy."

A hibiscus-tea package reads: "Tread and used for tea are the dried purely sepals of flowers, which are normally red or dark red colored and rather thick. In color of Hibiscus is very beautiful like a ruby red and its soft acidity is purely natural. Hibiscus has no stimlus as caffein, it will be highly recommended without anxiety to these from children to old men or to those who are sick in stomach or weakful." We are further assured that there are no "artificial coloring and appendixes contained."

A health drink is "made from the natural source and sometimes something appears on the surface but never mind. Shake it well and take it." Less beneficial, perhaps, but more palatable, is the vinegar and honey concoction which recommends that you add "a few drips of liquor, rum, brandy, and other alcohol" to it.

One beer slogan says: "The legendary Kirin is a

symbol of good luck. Open up Kirin today and you'll see what it's all about." But that's mild compared to: "Fly with Kirin on a voyage of discovery. Up through the clouds and into the heavens. Past the moon and the sun, the planets and the stars, into a land of taste experiences you'll never forget."

More restrained, another brand says: "The superior filtration method and total microorganisms control gave birth to Sapporo draft beer."

One canned drink says: "Select carefully raw material finished up splendifirous taste of ume drink." Another says: "Pokka white sour is refreshing and white like Alpine snow. Its sour taste of yogurt will extend on your tongue softly and be a sweetheart."

A third drink declares: "There is a gallon of de-

liciousness in every drop. Reach for the taste of good taste. Your ticket to drink paradise."

All this talk of drink reminds me of a postcard of the famed bullfights on the island of Shikoku. These are held six times a year, with the bulls pitted against each other in a show of strength. The winner is the one who drives his opponent from the ring. The explanation in English on the back of the card begins, "Before the bull fight, the bulls consume 20 eggs and a dozen beers to excite." The friend who sent the card comments: "If I had 20 eggs and a dozen beers, I bet *I'd* excite, too!"

— 10 —
You Want It, We Had It

JAPAN IS synonymous with service. Perhaps the people of no other country give it so cheerfully, so unstintingly, so entirely without expectation of return. Service is one thing. The printed word, however, is another, and then things have a decided tendency to go awry.

Many years ago the naval attaché of the Canadian Embassy, whose surname was Lee, ordered a supply of name cards. He had specified that under his name should be printed "Canadian Forces Attaché." Well, back came the cards, and under his name, "Ree," was printed "Canadian Forces Attacks."

He received an apology redirecting blame, along the lines of this postcard sent by a jewelry-design school president: "Our apologies. . . . We believe you may have noticed the erroneous use of 'sail' instead of 'sale' in our leaflet. We wish to assure you that this was the printer's error but not ours. Thank you very much."

Printers may make some errors, but this sign on a supermarket bulletin board is handwritten: "Please ask a cashier to validate your memo before your stick on you board."

At least one young Japanese woman has offered her services, via such a bulletin board, as a "baby shitter."

One supermarket posts this sign: "Turkey, chicken and ram roll are in the frozen room. To our customers."

Another offers: "Nambu Kashiwa, a wild chicken, is well feeded long enough with only natural food

Butchering is our speciality
Glue no extra charge!

at wild yard, which makes their meat more heavier body, flavorful and enjoyable."

Yet another supermarket asks customers, "Please don't poke a hole to watermelon."

Other shops, other prohibitions: "Kindly refrain from hot dog and soft clean," and "No smoking. No allowed explosive."

One Tokyo shop offers "big chests." Another has "potted plants and shapely stones," while a third sells "precious goods, antiques, and dead stock."

Speaking of which, an antique shop has old sword-case decorations "made in tie crasp with our idea. Very good copy made small sord brade."

Here are a few other "missarenious" slogans:

Fashionabull. Men! We hope fleedom (in a men's shop).

In Hot Pursuit of Dainty (on a laundry truck).

Dress Up By Cleaning (in a dry cleaner's).

You Want It, We Had It (at an electronics shop).

All ours is your sincerity (at a real-estate agency).

From birds to elephants, your pets hospital (at a vet's).

A bridal shop offers "weeding gowns," while a kimono shop has "ancient boy's kimono about 120 years ago used by high cluss famoly for automun and winters."

Boutiques have seasonal sales, called "put on," "fresh fit," and "charming."

A barber offers "heads cutting ¥1,500. For bald men ¥900," while a beauty shop advertises "all staff British trained with both Foreign and Japan hair."

One shop, offering unknown services, is called "Nice Clap."

Some services have curious names. A motorcycle delivery service is "Tarzan," while a house removal van is "Captain Removal." A beauty shop is "Jaguar." A meat van says on it "Meat Parsonarity," while a minibus says "Brute Planning Tokyo." Another minibus belongs to the "High In Come Company."

One Christmas two Tokyo residents decided to send "smoked sermon" to their respective parents in the United States. The sending of "smoked sermon" involved a journey to a department store where the fish is first bought and then carried to the "Overseas packing counter." A sales clerk offered to carry the parcel to the "packing." So off set the customers, the clerk, and the fish. In and out of elevators they went, up and down the building, until at last the clerk had guided the customers triumphantly to the garage, where, he assumes, they were "packed."

✳ ✳ ✳

You never know what you'll find in the classified advertisements. That's one reason for reading them. The word "health" caught my eye in one column, so I read the pitch of a physical fitness program. Tucked into the vital information was: "Contents: Worming up, Fitness with music, sport massage, yoga, cooling down." Worming up? Sport massage? It sounds positively dangerous.

Of a couple of postcards that came to the house, one advertised "an exciting night sale Part II" and offered the "rearest chances" to buy computers. The other said on it: "SHINJUKU INDOOR ANT. MARKET." Without the explanation, in smaller print,

of "good buys in antiques and curios," you'd be hard put to know what an "Indoor Ant" was, even if you knew where or what Shinjuku was.

The next advertisement is completely baffling: "Blue Sky. Cultural envoy networking the world. We will cultivate a reliable and fruitful living culture to contribute to the boundless development of human beings."

A brochure for a cruise glorifies the ship's facilities, the food, the scenery. It ends its pitch with the sincere assurance: "it really worths the money you pay." Let's hope so.

A Kyoto shop offers this guarantee to its customers: "If you are dissatisfied with our goods, please make you feel free to claim us or send the goods back without hesitation." It gives an all-encompassing guarantee of its products—"against the quality all the times."

In similar vein is this offer: "Thank you very much for your buying this. We make sure for quality control but if you become aware of changing in quality, etc. please you change at the shop which you bought in, or trouble you to send to our company. We change it and bear that the postage."

A shop gives this explanation for hiking its prices: "Recent big changes in conversion rate on the world currency exchange market forced us to adjust our prices at last. Please kindly understand that this amendment is merely occured to by above vital power which is beyond our control, not by the rising cost."

A much blunter message is this, for a Chinese carpet marked down to ¥380,000: "You cannot reasonably wish for more reduce the price."

Advertising assaults us in our daily lives. There are the luxuries, of course—the electronic and video equipment, the exclusive sports facilities, the holiday resorts. The basics, though—food, shelter, clothing—are never neglected. Just because we wear clothes each day doesn't mean that we can be trusted to choose the right ones without a little guidance. Advertising, therefore, never lets up.

A tailor sends out an advertisement offering discounts on his line of "BIG LAY Order Suit."

A sportswear shop puts out a cyclist's face mask called a "crow musk."

And a clothing shop promotes a shirt with these words: "It should be done at once if at all. Just fit your size. Large 16½."

Before you wear clothes with extraordinary messages on them, you'll find plenty of amusement just reading about them.

A robe is "all purpose home wear. It's extra comfortable and convenient for 7–11 (living) and also perfect for 11–7 (sleeping). Also for getting up to see if there is a burglar, raiding the icebox, eating breakfast, answering the doorbells, watching t.v., brushing your teeth, and combing your beard."

A sweater is advertised as: "Young casual knit. This line is made up in pursuit of fresh feeling and noble sense, and finished especially standing on the user's side."

A bra promises: "For your real satisfaction with your body fashion, now Triumph Nook can give you the one you've been looking for. . . . As a fashionable boutique specialized in women's inner wears, we proudly offer you our selected foundations and lingeries . . . especially those of directly imported from Europe with a rich variety for your body make-up will give you the real satisfaction that you've never got in Japan."

Magazines often concoct their own vocabulary. In one, "freshers" are "newly graduated business persons." The magazine then proceeds to lay down the law on a dress code for freshers: "Imagine one girl with a splendid jacket. If her shoes were not in harmony with it, only the unbalance will attract the eyes of others. Just like that, wearing a fancy shoes for commuting and change to sandals in office is really insensible. It's like wearing sandals for a dinner suit."

There's more on the subject of shoes: "It is said that the middle-heeled one, about 5 to 6 cm. in black or brown is most acceptable but beige is also good as it harmonizes with most colors. Of course lowheeled shoes are also good if you have enough courage to walk vividly in them."

Further guidelines for fashionable feet come from a shoe shop. Its advertisement reads:

> Your charm and d-andyism is began from feet.
> All time all seasons,KAMIKURI's shoes moody up your dream wear.

Finally, a friend goes to a tailor who advertises his suits as "easy fit." The tailor looks at my friend, shakes his head and says, "Oh, sir. You are semi-fat. Not easy fit."

— 11 —
Cheep Chic

You CANNOT HELP but wonder why young Japanese men and women choose the T-shirts, jackets, and sweaters that they do. You know the ones I mean, those with English words on them. They can't select them because they like the messages, not when the messages are hopelessly garbled. And when the phrases are downright rude—well, surely the wearers can't know what they mean?

I am positively embarrassed to report that at least one Japanese teenage girl is wandering around with "Want to pat my pussy" written boldly across her chest. A bikini-clad girl on the beach has "the torrid zone" written across her bottom. Another girl, this one in shorts, has "Bully Club, have a good time" scribbled across hers.

Imagine going anywhere with the words, "Green Bay Peckers" or "Philadelphia Sexers" or "Enjoy naked sports" inscribed on your shirt. Or even worse, this: "Mr. Zog's sex wax. Never spoils. It's best for your stick," inscribed on your shirt. Or "I love every bone in your body, especially mine." Or "Mental Disea's Surf Team." Or "Pestigious Image for young men since 1971."

One T-shirt smiles, "Lusty Bunny." Another beams, "Cheerful Cry Baby." A third exclaims, "She likes every music, including noises."

A T-shirt smirks: "Horoscope since 1959. We will dedicated to our lovers. Fresh-caught frisky sences." A shirt simpers: "Kookie Diana. She was still child enough to finally put the troubling thoughts out of her mind."

And what about: "Pinkish girl." "Sincerely thick. 1960. Think Deeply About Simple in a Moment." "A drop of precious sweat for your guts is filling the whole body. Play as eagerly as you can. Adidas gives earnest play to the hearty applause."

A sweater bears these astonishing words: "A. Flasher. Charge-a-date plan."

Blue jeans are called "pu push."

A jacket chants: "Midget boy. 440 yards. 1957," while another shouts, "Southall eis crewsing for rising sun with following blows."

Finally, one T-shirt sums them all up. It says, "CHEEP CHIC."

*   *   *

It's not just clothes that have strange messages written on them in English. Aprons do too, as do towels, curtains, and tablecloths.

Two aprons sit side by side on a department store shelf. One suggests that you "hop on the back of a big roving whale and you will go places boy such far away dreams." The other invites you to "take a swing on the man on the moon till you are up and away lost among the stars." What *can* they mean?

Both aprons and towels have such messages as "Love is harmony in the nature spreads out unlimitedly," "Hellow sports. Our hope is the forest or the plateau," and "Itsy Bitsy Buddies. It's so nice to chum up."

Here's a virtual short story, written on a towel: "Cattle Family. My farm stands on a little green hill. A crean stream runs just in the middle of the farm and various kinds of small animals play around there. The place full of fresh air and greens, it's Milk Land. The milk from this farm is excellent. Look at me. So healthy."

Here's another: "Sweet Fresh. We make vegetables from fantastic dreams. Plesent create studio carrot radish and lovely corn for health. Plesent create studio Wood Song Fresh Fop. Sunny days, dancing heart, Milk boy humming."

This towel has a short, sweet message: "Cotton feather have you with simple mind."

Move on to animals and you could have a towel that says "Adult duck. Crazy love. Grassland and lake," or "Antique bear, be happy. Heartful present," or "Be happy. 1914. Crazy love. Natural." This last has a picture of a long-eared rabbit wearing a chintz dress.

Finally, could you wash your face with a towel that has a picture of a cow—the back view of a cow wearing pink underpants, that is—and the legend "Milky Mate—Fanny Palette"?

Carrier bags with obscure messages are a subject unto themselves. Some are handed to you to contain your purchases. Sturdier ones are on sale. Some long-time residents here have large enough collections to supply entire shops. I remember a theme party where everyone was required to bring the looniest bag findable. Many a message makes no sense whatever, although a few can be reasonably entertaining. "Little Jammy and Christopher," for one. "Harajuku, mecca of dude, dundy, or fop," for another.

A shop says, via its shopping bag, that it is the "intersection of worldwide flavors and friendship." Others have such inspirational messages as:

California had better to live in the nature I think so.

We can't fly like a bird but we can have a free wing in our mind.

Produced by Hello Juicy.

The exciting couple of animals.

Now baby. Tonight I am feeling cool and hard boiled.

Let's sports violent all day long.

ELEPHANT DUM IS A POPULAR WITH
US. HIS HUMMING MAKES US
FEEL DANCING LIKE A
CONJURING TRICK.

St. Louis. That gal got a heart like a rock cast in
the sea.
For the young and the young at heat.
How about sharing company? Let's Chat, Pop-
corn shared will become fluffy white clouds.
And a friend can turn your Insides into a Clear
Blue Sky.
This word keeps pupping through my mind.
Handling elegance.
Pineapple Samba Wao! Cause Music is tight and
feel so high just be free.

Being alone. 1,000 miles far away. So please write
to put the silver lining behind my cloud.

You are too important to have ugly pockets. Slim
down and feel younger with the bag.

As the sun sparkled again, tears subsided. Time
has come for another to shine.

Passion. It visits on a lifetime. As if a shower is
passing.

Survival chic. As old wood is best to burn, old
horse to ride, old books to read, and old wine to
drink, so are old friends always most trusty to
use.

You shall have anyting you want, if you carry
this bag.

*　　*　　*

The entertainment world is not without its . . .
entertainment. A theater announces, "All tent total
on the border to the place of ice firing."

A movie poster says: "It's was presented to sensible people. In fantastic and with entertaining. The
splendid movies is open at this autumn." A synopsis
of one "splendid movie" describes a patient being
carried on a stretcher as "a stretch case."

A magazine heralds a festival: "Good and old
American music will be playing in the park all the
time. It's a festival that you can find full of 'sneakers'
feeling there." What could a "sneakers" feeling be,
I want to know.

An interview with an entertainer says that "he
tries to besiege the audience in gorgeous mood,"

and that "he is one of very rare entertainers in Japan."
According to him, "the shows must be enjoyable."

A postcard advertises a disco: "Let's dance good
moody music like 'Thanks Goods it's Friday.'"

To commemorate an anniversary, a disco, grandly
named White House, sends a letter:

White House is for people who thinks discoteque:
—is for wild young people with no taste for elegance.
—is noisy. It's too cheap a place to visit with a
  boy-friend.
—Services are poor and no high-class guests
  around. It's no place for me.
—Why, my time to have a bottle of whiskey kept
  must have expired?
These are no longer your worry at White House.
At White House you will enjoy the atmosphere of
a party of matured people in luxurious interior
settings—and with dericious cuisines, and the most
courteous treatment.

The couples whose first moment of encounter
in life was at White House keep writing us that
they're living the happiest life. White House and
its staff are proud of their role as Cupids or silent
guardians of young love romance.

White House is fashionable world of sound
where you will love to spend your time of relaxation.

It is suggested that you come to White House in

clothes that would fit the atmosphere of White House just as other guests do.

We wait for you, and bring your friends, too.

Next thing you know, "Alfalfa" sends a "Party Ticket" with the stark information: "We don't go discotequing anymore, because it's out now. What an 'in' thing this party is! Why don't you stay overnight? Bottoms up!"

There's plenty more to read on this small ticket. "We're gonna give a party that day, just tell us when your stomach's empty. We'll fill it with delicious foods, drinks, and nice conversation."

As for your heart: "We'll fill it with love and nice music."

The muddled words babble on: "Be nice, will you? Empty your dish before you ask for a second helping, and don't speak with your mouth full. Warning: No life guard on duty. Drink at your own risk."

The end, believe it or not, is a jaunty "Satisfaction guaranteed."

*   *   *

The Japanese have a penchant for adopting, then abbreviating, English words. As a matter of course, a department store becomes a "depaato," a supermarket a "soopa." So we really shouldn't blink when condominiums are advertised as "condoms."

Many advertisements aim first at improving your

accommodation. A brochure from a brand new apartment building promises: "Your better life will be guaranteed by such an extraordinary best location, facility, appliances and arrangement." It gives a "qualified floor plan" and concludes with "Furthermore, all your stuffs can be stored in the big closets."

After you're installed in your "extraordinary best location" you should investigate some frills. A cable radio network sends out a strange pamphlet that says "good news to your life from the cable radio." It offers "music news and information whenever you like it amazing"!

The blurb, with odd hyphenation of words intact, goes:

HELLOW, EVERYBODY OF FOREIGN RESIDENTS I
-N JAPAN. WE ARE THE CORPORATION OF MUSI
-C SUPPLY, TO WORK OFFICE OR SHOP AND TO
AT HOME. AND NOW, WE DEVELOPED THE SPECIA
-L PROGRAMS FOR FOREIGNER IN JAPAN STAY.
THE CONTENTS IS, IT HAVE AND HOLD AS DISK
JOCKY PROGRAMS OF ENGLISH EDITION FAR JA
-PANESE FORK SONGS 320 KINDS. AND IT IS,
YOU CAN CHOOSE IN FREEDOM. BESIDES, IT IS
EVERYDAY OR EVERYTIME.
WE SAY, LET'S LISTEN YOUR EARS OF JAPANE
-SE TASTES.

A company selling VHS and BETA tapes sends a questionnaire that begins: "A Letter of Request. I

ask you to record the American TV programs instead I do that. I amuse it myself and I never use it
for any other purpose."

A carpet company sends a soliciting letter, promot-
ing a product to stabilize loose rugs and small car-
pets. Their product is called "carpet creep stop
sheet" and this is the letter:

> Problem solver from A-1 Carpet Company, Ltd.
> Carpet Creep Stop Sheet for piece carpets or
> rugs. If you are having a trouble for keeping
> your rugs laid on carpets from creeping, we
> have a right product to solve your problem. Our
> Carpet Creep Stop Sheet prevents rugs laid on
> carpets from creeping.
> If you have a similar product already, don't
> stick with your brand, 'stick' with ours like our
> Carpet Creep Stop Sheet sticks between rugs
> and carpets. The remainder pieces can be used
> for your friends as a sample to surprise them
> how sticky Carpet Creep Stop Sheet is.

The carpet company is a member in good standing
of the Association of Interior Decor Specialists,
which, believe it or not, still calls itself "AIDS International, U.S.A."

*   *   *

An American businessman who spent a chunk of
his formative years in Tokyo has kept a letter from
that earlier time. Here it is, word for phonetically
misspelled word:

Tanaka Electlic Co.
For your benefit!

We had been walking for 15 years, at the sells department.

Cheeply, Swiftly
(short turm),

These are our belief! Did you have the trouble by the telephone? If you so, Immediately Call us. Absoletly, we will fly to your appointment in any occation.

Any-how, We are telephones professional and consultant. May I consult in any case for the telecominucation and electlic.

For, our shops has been living on for the 20 years.

As we have been getting trust by the everybody and anywhere.

We treat one for telephone, Swishborde, those parts, air-condition, interphone, wire-less cominucation, car-stereo, amprifair, TV-set, ice-box, radio, tereco, azc. . . . .

Thank you, sir, but I think I must take off now. Good-bye, our dear guest.

For the present, I will to see you latter on.

Just for fun, when he returned to Tokyo as an adult, the businessman dialed the old number of the Tanaka Electlic Company. Would you believe that the voice at the other end of the phone boomed, "Tanaka!" Still going strong!

— 12 —
Nail Remover

ONCE UPON A TIME someone had the bright idea of labeling goods with the English word "my." It was supposed to add a personal touch. The Japanese happily adopted the word and used it in many situations.

"Now let's return to 'my' office," says the Japanese subordinate to the Western boss (who owns the company, by the way) after they have lunched together and are to return to the office. Said subordinate also drives "my car" and smokes "my cigarettes."

In fact, there are whole lines of goods with slogans beginning with "my." Most are innocuous, like the skipping rope called "My Jump" and clotheslines and scrubbing brushes called "My Green Life." Others take a more positive line. A vending machine says: "Toothbrash bending machine. Good days, good foods, good my life."

Then, almost inevitably, come the clangers. A bank comes out with "My Bank, My Kinki." And Tokyo Gas concocts "My Life, My Gas."

Then there's the toilet paper called "My Fanny."

Where else in the world would babies' diapers be called "My Pee"? And while we're on the subject, there's even a teakettle around called a "pee pee pot."

You can fill your home to overflowing with all manner of curiously labeled items. A washer is a "free size twinkle tap." Air fresheners come in four varieties: "Be free from care as a butterfly," "Don't

be flurried as a little fish," "Keep a clean life as a racoon," and "Wake up early as a bird."

Prepare your dinner with a "rice cocker" and clean your teeth afterward with toothpicks called "dent peckers." Blow your nose with "cool sniffies" tissues.

An electronic bicycle horn comes equipped with a "sportlight, siren alarm and AM radio ideal for all purpose indoor, outdoor, and power failure."

The instructions say: "Usages when your turn on the radio keep the switch off. Turn on the volume and selector. Whatever the Radio is On or Off. Siren Alarm can be obtained by putting the switch downward and the Horn can be achieved by pressing the Horn Button. Sportlight can be gained by putting the switch upward."

Add Halloween decorations to your holiday reading. The mug says: "Halloween, Studio Corgi Collection Vol. I. Bow-wow and his friends enjoy the Halloween party. They say 'Tricks or treats?'

each other in the dark." And the plate goes further: "Halloween. Studio Corgi Collection Vol. I. Everyone will enjoy Halloween party. In a dark, many witches and bats will enjoy, too."

Other ornaments have year-round application. The wall plaque, for instance, that says: "Their splendid house here we have excellent air and eating. Peoples awake by dirds' singing every morning. Peoples see beautiful spring bloom. Peoples can play at river in summer and go nutting in fall. Peoples eat hot foods beside stove. Peoples enjoy best living around here through the year. They are living a full life every day. Wonderful place."

Another wall plaque shows on it a couple standing by a bus stop. In the background are a building and a car. Inscribed are the words, "Another Scene. Man and Lady, meet this town. Then they have meltting mood. This town called love lorn town."

Many goods that find their way on to the consumer shelves in Japan might well feel naked without packaging in English as well as in Japanese. Imported items often inspire advertising campaigns

another scene.
man and lady, meet this town.
then they have meltting mood.
this town called love lorn town.

geared only to the local consumer. But really, where else other than in Japan would a cosmetics company even *think* of advertising a face cream called "Visible Difference" by its initials? Fortunately, an English person in the company squashed that idea.

Still, there is "peculiar cold cream" on the market, and a cleansing cream that "cleanses skin out of deep pores." Poor skin!

A nail care product is "for male and female, young and old. Please share the joy of having one's own natural shine with your family." Polish remover is called "nail remover." One application only, presumably.

A hair spray's slogan is "Hair up blow." A hair gel comes in three varieties: "Miss Party." "More Setten," and "Wet Pose."

A hair tonic "sinks deep into the scalp and transfer energy to assist the renewal of protein in the cells, where our body fail to do normally in time. Terminal hair grows within a short time." Wisely, the manufacturers don't attempt to substantiate this claim.

Tidy your hair with a "free and free brushing brush." A comb says "any time, any hair." Another comb is a "hand made high class comb. The fruit of technique produced by leading comb maker HIGH CLASS COMB old in experience. Good for your hair and easy to use, especially tooth being made up cavefully with a special method. So, you can dress your hair comfortably every day."

The packet of a toothbrush reads, "Oh yes! Find out nice feeling!"

Sachets say: "A perfume accessory for sensible ladies. Surely fit you. Certainly you like veiling in dreamy fragrance. Also best for a acceptable present."

Bath salts come with the casual instructions, "Dissolve 2½ spoons in your bath."

A washcloth called "Clean Clean" identifies itself as "a magic towel for health and beauty" and goes on to say "enjoy tenderness and softness to your skin. Sure! Best for beathing and massage. Economical! Yes, you can save ½ soap with Clean Clean. Healthy! Tender stimulation will make a better blood circulation and make your skin more charming and blooming."

A "Decorative Towel" says: "You can use this towel in many ways. It's up to you! Let it perk up various places . . . for example please use it as interior decoration, lap robe, sheet for children, cover for car seat, for bed ridden patients use over the pillow or sheet to avoid soiled sheet."

Cotton gauze, meanwhile, comes in a package with these directions: "Stretching it for cleansing, folding it for patting."

Finally, there's a bronzing oil that "makes you wild and sexy." Three bottles, please.

— 13 —
Please Enjoy Her Pathetic Voice

MANY A JAPANESE COMPANY hires a "native speaker" to cope with their English-language correspondence and to correct their English-language promotions. Such work has its moments. For instance, a French chanson singer is touring Japan. Press releases are submitted to an American for his approval. He realizes at once, of course, that she is being praised, that she sings soulful renditions of sad ballads. The sentence he stares at, however, implores: "Please enjoy her pathetic voice."

A brochure on a burglar alarm system called "Watch Dog" begins: "This is an all transistorised automatic radio wave alarm devised for the first time by us."

It then describes "various alarming devises." To begin with: "The first alarming is made at once by the alarm lamp which projects a menacing light on the invader in the dark." If that isn't sufficient deterrent, "an invader steps within this spherical area, regardless of the angle and direction the radio wave is disturbed and the electro-magnetic wave produced by the phase difference in the frequency of the radio wave caused by the reflection to the eradiated wave on the invader is transmitted back to the master unit."

"Watch Dog" is so clever that "the delayed action system and unsuitable alarming due to small animals is eliminated." Happily, furthermore, "Watch Dog can be placed in a room without spoiling the atmosphere."

Now let's move on to real animals. A translation

of a speech about the future of riding and horse breeding in Japan contains this sentence: "In foreign countries they get a good blood colt with chearper cost and bleed him good." The translation also mentions "stuck bleeders"—more commonly known as stock breeders!

*   *   *

A Japanese airline executive is asked to give a talk in English at an international seminar. He is to make suggestions to smooth the way for the increasing numbers of Japanese first-time travelers. He jots down the points he wants to make, then asks for assistance in the actual writing.

He starts with observations of what Japanese visitors to New Zealand are up against: "Agricultural declaration form increase Japanese clearly explained why such a form has to be completed. I strongly feel the content of the questionnaire give a very peculiar impression to Japanese visitors. I knew one Japanese lady had chewing gam conficicated and could not understand the reason."

Another point he makes about food is: "I must say that a kind explanation of variety of food which will be served particularly on-tray, dinner time are necessary to Japanese. In Japan very seldom will you be asked to have on-tray before the main table food, and since you have many variety of decoration, recommendation of the waitress will also be very much appreciated."

He ends with a remark about needing to overcome the "language burrier."

His sentiment was echoed by a British hostess at a cocktail party. She asked a Japanese guest, who happened to be a professor of literature, "Do you care for a sherry?"

He replied, "I prefer Keats," and they stared at each other, one baffled by the question, the other by the answer.

But to return to the written word, while staying with the scholarly theme, the chancellor of a Japanese university prepared this message for a special

occasion: "As one of Old Boys of the E.S.S. I do heartily welcome all of you and congratulate on this Grand Meeting. I was an earnest and eager student of this society nearly 50 years ago. I hope that all of you who assembled on this occasion, try hard and do success in every part you purpose. Boys be ambitious, because it is said that you expect a lumber and get a tiny pine. But be deligent and practical, as visions are visions and never get a pout if you only dreamed it. Congratulations on the success of this Grand Meeting."

E.S.S. stands for English Speaking Society. I venture to suppose that most Japanese high schools and universities have one. It's a revelation to know they were around before the war.

Students produce their share of howlers. In a dictation lesson, a teacher dwells on crime prevention. Back comes an essay about "grime prevention."

Another teacher dictates to his class: "After the Meiji Restoration, Japan worked very hard to adopt Western methods of culture and technology."

One of his students carefully writes down: "After the Meiji Frustration, Japan worked very hard to adopt Western methods of torture and technology." You're tempted to think that his English is on a par with his teacher's and that he is having a bit of fun.

A third teacher tells his students that "the pen is mightier than the sword." Do I have to tell you what his students—one of them, anyway—records? "The penis mightier than the sword."

From the classroom to the office. A Japanese man,

on his return from his first trip to London, tells the Englishwoman in his office, "Thanks to your kind guidance, I could enjoy bitter beer in association with sausage rolls."

A young Japanese man, visiting a European's home, tells her, "Your house is very tasty." She regards him suspiciously, wondering if he's been gnawing the furniture.

An office girl writes a note and slides it over to a colleague's desk: "I'm going to patty. So would you watch my job for awhile? Patty means is rest room (bath room)."

Another young woman apologizes to a visitor for

a rainy day. "The weather today is very sorry," she says. And so it should be.

A third politely asks a tall American coworker, "How long are you?" In reply he blushes, probably for the first time in his adult life.

A Japanese student, in high school uniform, approaches a Western woman who is sitting in a Tokyo hotel lobby. "Sir," he says loudly, "I want to practice on you."

An American businessman blinks at the telephone message on his desk. It says, loud and clear, "Please to call Miss Susan. She is expecting." Then he remembers where he is, and picks up the phone without a qualm.

After years of dedication to her company, a secretary is moving on to a new job. She asks for a letter of recommendation. This is what she receives: "Miss Suzuki has worked for our company for 14 years. She is leaving at the end of the month. We are very satisfied."

— 14 —
Potato Girl and Radish Baby

I HAVE HEARD it said that when some companies are deciding which words should cover their shirts, bags, or whatever, they first pick them—at random? or are these decisions made at executive level?—and then hand them to copywriters to weave together. This could explain how some words with nothing in common come to be joined in eternal wedlock.

Wherever the words originate, there's always a lot to read in stationers' shops. Shelves of stationery have messages written in English. Some are short and sweet, such as "Shine more beautifully and gently," "That casual meeting with you has changed my destiny so greatly," and "We're strong and always full of vigor. Be Ambiscious!"

Your writing has to scorch and sizzle to justify a letterhead that says, "We keep on sending you hot messages." Or would you prefer paper that says, "Fashion mind beads new world. They have been elegant ladies with pure, sweet, and bitter memories."

Other stationery has so much to say that all you need do is sign your name and you've sent a letter: "Come whenever the day break, we always stair in the station at the outskirts of a town. Follow a map at the finger, search the train for we will be born again in the strange ground. Every time we want to something . . . and every time wait for something. Fill an empty grease bottle with a lot of dreams, I won't lose boyish heart forever."

Another long message says: "Story Boy and Girl Love Story Act I. Someday in the Downtown Street:

Kiss. After enjoying at the seashore let's have a tea time being affected little bit. Meg is eating her favourite Petit-beurre and drinking milk tea. Jun is drinking a cup of black coffee giving himself not having a coke as usual. Both of them are enjoying an adult mood." And you'll have to come up with an adult message to follow that!

A letter writing-pad called "Happy" declares: "This writing Pad is an excellent example of Japanese traditional paper with modern technique of beautiful 'water mark' combined. This can be a Cupid for you, conveying Love and Happiness to your friend. Your beautiful Heart will surely be better expressed by this elegant letter paper. Also we would recommend this for your invitatory and congratulatory letter so that most splendid atmosphere might be created."

A notebook says on its cover: "Memories of what once was, the sentimental fool, a tear, his only comfort his bag of Ebi-sen." Ebi-sen is a shrimp-flavored Japanese cracker, so this is not the notebook for weight watchers. Fancy suggesting—no, encouraging—eating for comfort, and for your only comfort, at that!

Another notebook says, "Potato girl. This potato is a lovely girl," while a similar one proclaims, "Radish baby. This radish is a merry baby."

A notebook with baseball terms all over its cover includes the phrase "antsy pants." Another says: "Looking out of a window a gentle breeze smooth my muzzle. This is the secret land where there is

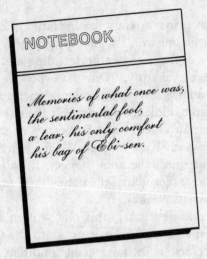

NOTEBOOK

Memories of what once was,
the sentimental fool,
a tear, his only comfort
his bag of Ebi-sen.

no sound." I suspect that the author of that phrase concocted it because he was being blasted by those familiar Tokyo sounds: traffic, road construction, and loudspeakers.

File notecards, in 5″ × 3″ size, are called "mini intelligence cards." Just what every executive needs.

Then there's the "Team-Demi" of miniature-sized office supplies, the case of which says: "To make your life more pleasant. Take it with you."

* * *

A lifetime in Japan, a lifetime of collecting charming letters. A yellowing one in an old file is dated 1951. It is from a Japanese man who is making his first overseas trip. It is to New Zealand to investigate the possibilities of importing New Zealand horses into Japan.

"This is my first attempt writing letter in English," he begins his missive. "I am just going to write it taking my courage as like horse riding and jump."

He goes on, chattily, "One day when we were in kinema and we saw your Emperor picture on the screen. Large audience stoop up at their seat. I felt it very comfortable." "My Emperor" at that time must have been King George VI, for it was before the present queen became "Queen Elizabath II." She and her father shared the same "Prim Minister," Sir Winston Churchill.

Another horsey letter, this one written in 1956, is from Japan's equestrian entrant to the Olympic Games. "Horse is in quite good condition and the voyage seems to suffer him nothing. Although sometimes he jumps a little bigger than I expect but I should like to be as man and wife until Olympic Game, not in a hurry."

Years later, this same man writes of a partnership with another horse. "I'm still struggling with my mare under the burning sun with hopeless hope."

Later yet he remarks, "The organization has no rule now. Regulations in programs were scrutched and one man rules and all others were never against him. He is one of those mountaintoper."

Another letter arrives from another Japanese man on an overseas trip. Horrified at his schedule, he says, "Oh, my every muscle is wanting something like spinach though I'm not Popi."

A Japanese company head sends a congratulatory telegram to an Alaskan senator:

I HOPE YOUR MARRIAGE WILL STRENGTHEN AND
INCREASE YOUR ENTHUSIASM AND VIGOR FOR
YOUR ACTIVITIES, ESPECIALLY ALASKA-JAPAN
LINKAGE. AS A SINO-JAPANESE PROVERBS SAYS,
IN THE MARRIAGE, GO-BETWEEN IS CALLED
GENTLEMAN ON THE ICE OF THE WATER IN THE
MOONLIGHT. WE ARE LOOKING FORWARD TO
SEEING YOUR WIFE AND YOU IN TOKYO AS THE
LADY AND GENTLEMAN OF THE ICE OF THE WATER
OF THE PACIFIC IN THE BEAUTIFUL MOONLIGHT.

All that, on a telegram!

My mother, whose name is Vivienne, gives her
name over the telephone to a man who is to send
a pamphlet. She wonders at the ease with which he
accepts her name and concludes that he must be a
movie buff, familiar with Vivien Leigh.

Well, the pamphlet arrives all right—in an en-
velope addressed to "B.B.N. Kenlik." In Japan
"v's" and "b's" are as interchangeable as are
"l's" and "r's."

To underline this, let me tell you about a multi-
lingual friend of mine who telephones a Tokyo hotel.
He wants to reach a visitor from Greece, a man with
the surname of Lemos.

"Is that 'L' as in Rome?" asks the Japanese voice
at the other end of the line.

"No," replies my quick-witted friend. "It's 'R' as in London."

And, believe it or not, he is put straight through to Mr. Lemos.

*　　*　　*

I shall end by returning to the Ocean Expo in Okinawa. Many a press release, letter, and invitation circulated during those months. A letter of introduction said: "It gives you great pleasure to introduce me to you as the new Pavilion Manager."

The Japanese manager of one of the pavilions churned out a steady volume of news releases and letters. His jovial personality came across on paper as strongly as it did in person.

One of his earliest letters was an open invitation to visit him: "It is very happy to inform you that we welcome anytime, whenever you and your guests wish to visit us. That time, please phone extension 582 before your visit, otherwise, we may give you heavy trouble when you come to us. Waiting for your nice courtesy call."

Then came an expansive invitation. "Dear Sir: We would like to hold a cocktail party with foreign and Japanese participants for the purpose of becoming intimate with each other."

Finally, he circularized this thank you: "It is my best pleasure that my mother and wife been entertained well from your heartfull hospitality during their visit. Surely they have enjoyed too much and naturally must be kept in memory forever."

Miranda Kenrick has been collecting and chuckling over Japanized English since her school days in Tokyo. She has lived there all her life, a permanent resident in a transient society. Traveling is Miranda's passion, and she has been to over 110 countries, going overland whenever possible. She has written for a number of newspapers and magazines, and was coauthor of *Too Far East Too Long*, the story of her first 30 years in Japan. Miranda has been involved for many years, on the boards and behind the scenes, with Tokyo's community theatre group, the Tokyo International Players.